THE LI...

by

JOHN N MERRILL

Maps and Photographs by John N. Merrill

a J.N.M. PUBLICATION

1989

i

a J.N.M. PUBLICATION

JNM PUBLICATIONS,
WINSTER,
MATLOCK,
DERBYSHIRE.
DE4 2DQ

Conceived, edited, typeset, designed, marketed and distributed by John N. Merrill.

© Text and routes — John N. Merrill 1969 and 1989

© Maps and photographs — John N. Merrill 1989

First Published — December 1969
Reprinted 1976 and enlarged in February 1983
This revised edition — March 1989

ISBN 0 907496 83 0

Meticulous research has been undertaken to ensure that this publication is highly accurate at the time of going to press. The publishers, however, cannot be held responsible for alterations, errors or omissions, but they would welcome notification of such for future editions.

Printed by: Elgar Printing Ltd

Set in Futura — Medium and bold.

Front cover sketch — Lathkill Dale from Conksbury Bridge by John Creber. © JNM Publications.

Back cover map — © JNM Publications.

ABOUT JOHN N. MERRILL

John combines the characteristics and strength of a mountain climber with the stamina and athletic capabilities of a marathon runner. In this respect he is unique and has to his credit a whole string of remarkable long walks. He is without question the world's leading marathon walker.

Over the last fifteen years he has walked more than 100,000 miles and successfully completed ten walks of at least 1,000 miles or more.

His six major walks in Great Britain are -
Hebridean Journey .... 1,003 miles
Northern Isles Journey .... 913 miles
Irish Island Journey .... 1,578 miles
Parkland Journey .... 2,043 miles
Lands End to John o'Groats... 1,608 miles
and in 1978 he became the first person (permanent Guinness Book of Records entry) to walk the entire coastline of Britain — 6,824 miles in ten months.

In Europe he has walked across Austria — 712 miles — hiked the Tour of Mont Blanc, completed High Level Routes in the Dolomites and Italian Alps, and the GR20 route across Corsica in training! In 1982 he walked across Europe — 2,806 miles in 107 days — crossing seven countries, the Swiss and French Alps and the complete Pyrennean chain — the hardest and longest mountain walk in Europe, with more than 600,000 feet of ascent!

In America he used the the world's longest footpath — The Appalachian Trail -2,200 miles — as a training walk. He has walked from Mexico to Canada via the Pacific Crest Trail in record time — 118 days for 2,700 miles. In Canada he has walked the Rideau Trail.

During the summer of 1984, John set off from Virginia Beach on the Atlantic coast, and walked 4,226 miles without a rest day, across the width of America to Santa Cruz and San Francisco on the Pacific Ocean. His walk is unquestionably his greatest achievement, being, in modern history, the longest, hardest crossing of the USA in the shortest time — under six months (178 days). The direct distance is 2,800 miles.

Between major walks John is out training in his own area — the Peak District National Park. As well as walking in other parts of Britain and Europe he has been trekking in the Himalayas five times. He has created more than ten challenge walks which have been used to raise more than £250,000 for charity. From his own walks he raised over £80,000. He is author of more than ninety books, most of which he publishes himself. His book sales are in excess of 2 million.

CONTENTS

CAVE DALE — IN WINTER

iv

INTRODUCTION

Running almost from the end of the Pennine Way, in a north to south direction to the 'Derbyshire plain', is an extensive limestone dale system. Lovers of the Peak District will know of Dovedale and Monsal Dale, but there are more than 100 other ones. In June 1969 I set off from Castleton, the northernmost outcrop of limestone, and walked south via 18 dales to Dovedale.

I was immediately struck by the beauty of the different dales. Some had swift-flowing rivers with steep limestone buttress sides. Others were dry and more open, but always with lush vegetation and an abundance of wildlife and a profusion of flowers. Surprisingly, apart from Monsal Dale and Dovedale, I saw no-one and enjoyed a long walk away from the cares and worries of modern life.

The 1970s saw a rapid growth in walking, and many people wrote to me asking for a route to walk as a challenge. I amended my original route, for it was now possible to walk through other dales which originally had no right of way, such as Monks' Dale. Rather than end the walk at Dovedale I decided, masochistically, to end at Thorpe, thus including a 20th dale but also a climb at the end of a forty-mile walk.

Since my first book on the walk I have received hundreds of letters from people who followed my footsteps. Thankfully, all the letters have been complimentary! In this book I have totally upgraded all the information and walking instructions, hopefully making it even easier to walk. The maps are totally new and should give even greater details of the route.

The walk is still one of my favourites, and one that I walk at least once a year in training! Whilst many people complete the walk in a day, 15 hours, there is no urgency to do so. There are hostels, campsites, and bed and breakfast establishments on or close to the route, making the walk a very enjoyable weekend walk. However you do it, and whatever season, I hope you enjoy walking down some of England's choicest scenery.

Happy walking!

John N. Merrill.

John N. Merrill
Winster.

P.S. I had a letter recently from someone who had walked the Limey Way. He left Castleton on Saturday morning and reached Thorpe that evening. He had enjoyed it so much that he walked back to Castleton the next day! Some even combine my Limey Way and Rivers' Way together, making a magnificent 90 mile circular walk.

HOW TO DO IT

The route is covered by the following Ordnance Survey maps:-

1:25,000 Series — Outdoor Leisure map — The White Peak.
1:50,000 Series — Sheet No. 110 — Sheffield and Huddersfield.
Sheet No. 119 — Buxton, Matlock and Dovedale.

Most people walk the route in 24 hours and set off from Castleton from 6 a.m. onwards. The average time is 14/15 hours. There is no need to complete it in a day, and if 40 miles is too much for you then take two days and break the route at Monyash or Youlgreave. There is no easy way back from Thorpe to Castleton, and it is to be hoped that your back-up party or wife is there to drive you home to a delicious hot bath.

Back-up parties will find the route well traversed by rendezvous points. I would suggest that Millers Dale, White Lodge car park, Monyash, Alport, Dale End, Friden car park, Mill Dale and Thorpe are the logical meeting places for food and first-aid posts.

The summer months are the best time to walk the route, for the winter months mean short daylight hours and muddy ground. Hopefully your traverse will be on a hot, sunny day as you make your way down the dales. There are numerous inns en route to 'spur' you on your way. Whilst the walking is important, there is much flora and fauna to be seen, historical buildings and places of legend and murder to learn about.

The Youth Hostel at Youlgreave maintains a register for persons walking the route.

For those completing the walk, there are badges and completion certificates available from JNM Publications, a red badge for those successfully completing it within 24 hours, and a green badge for 48 hours. See badge order form at rear of book.

CAVE DALE AND PEVERIL CASTLE

ABOUT THE WALK -

Whilst every care is taken detailing and describing the walks in this book, it should be borne in mind that the countryside changes by the seasons and the work of man. I have described the walks to the best of my ability, detailing what I have found on the walk in the way of stiles and signs. Obviously with the passage of time stiles become broken or replaced by a ladder stile or even a small gate. Signs too have a habit of being broken or pushed over. All the routes follow rights of way and only on rare occasions will you have to overcome obstacles in its path, such as a barbed wire fence or electric fence.

The seasons bring occasional problems whilst out walking which should also be borne in mind. In the height of summer paths become overgrown and you will have to fight your way through in a few places. In low lying areas the fields are often full of crops, and although the pathline goes straight across it may be more practical to walk round the field edge to get to the next stile or gate. In summer the ground is generally dry but in autumn and winter, especially because of our climate, the surface can be decidedly wet and slippery; sometimes even glutonous mud!

These comments are part of countryside walking which help to make your walk more interesting or briefly frustrating. Standing in a farmyard up to your ankles in mud might not be funny at the time but upon reflection was one of the highlights of the walk!

VIEW TO CONIES DALE

3

CASTLETON TO MILLER'S DALE – 8 MILES

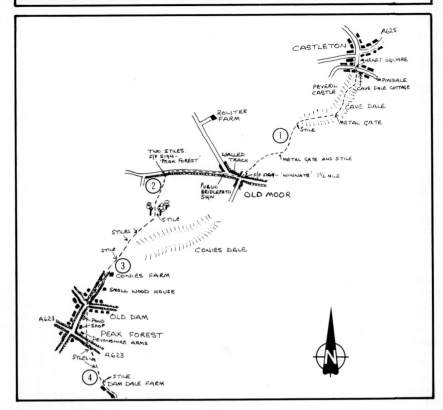

CASTLETON — A major tourist resort containing numerous items of interest. Dominating the village are the ruins of Peveril Castle, while below is the church dedicated to St. Edmund dating back to the Norman times with impressive chancel arch. In and around Castleton are several show caves — Peak Cavern with the largest cave entrance in Britain; Speedwell Cavern, whose stalactites are reached by a subterranean boat ride; Treak Cliff Cavern and Blue John Mine are nearby. Blue John stone is mined in the area; it is unique, and made locally into jewellery. On Oak Apple Day in late May a unique garland ceremony is held in the village and is believed to commemorate the restoration of Charles II.

PEVERIL CASTLE — Dates from the 11th Century, when the manor was given to William Peveril. The keep was built in 1176 at a cost of £135. Although the castle saw no fighting it was in use until the 15th Century.

PEAK FOREST — The church is dedicated to King Charles, King and Martyr. The present building dates from 1880 but the original chapel built in 1657 was the Midlands Gretna Green. Because Peak Forest did not come under the jurisdiction of any Bishop, the Vicar had the right to grant marriage licences. A 'Foreign Marriage' register was kept, and between 1728 — 1754 about 80 people a year were married here, without banns and at any hour of the day or night. Lord Hardwick's Act of 1754 put a stop to these runaway marriages.

CASTLETON TO MILLER'S DALE — 8 MILES

WALKING INSTRUCTIONS

Leave the Market Place by the top left road — Pindale Road. Almost immediately turn right inbetween Dale and Cavedale Cottages and begin walking up the path into Cave Dale, crossing a stile en route. Once in the dale, there are limestone buttresses on either side; high on your right are the ramparts of Peveril Castle. Continue along the wide path and begin a steep rocky ascent up the dale with impressive views back to the castle. In time you pass through a metal gate at the end of the main ascent. Follow the path to your right through a shallow dale with a wall on your left. The dale bears left to a metal gate and stile at a stone wall. Cross this to the next stile; after this take the lefthand track to a stile, walled track and footpath junction. Turn right as signposted for — Winnats 1 mile — and walk along a walled track. Where the track bears right 250 yards later, keep straight ahead on Public Bridlepath — a grass track with a wall on your left. Approximately half a mile later, now on a grass track, you reach a track and path 'T' junction. Here turn left and ascend two stiles, following the path signposted for 'Peak Forest'. Now you begin to descend and the pathline is faint; once over the brow of the field you can see a cluster of trees — head for these where there is a stile on the right, near the field boundary. Turn right through the trees and past the lead-mining remains. At the end of the trees turn left, following a faint path to a stile, with Conies Dale on your left in the bottom. At the stile bear right to the next, keeping the wall on your right. The path line is now obvious as you continue descending to the dale floor; the stiles beside the gates guide you. Gain the walled track beside Conies Farm and continue down it, passing Small Wood House on your left. At the road junction in Old Dam continue straight ahead towards Peak Forest. Almost immediately, turn left up a track to the stile on the right. Walk beside the wall on your left with the pond on your right. Ascend the stile on your left and pass the farm buildings to the next stile. At the next farm immediately afterwards, turn right and follow the farm road to your left to the A623 road. The Devonshire Arms Inn is on your right.

OLD DAM

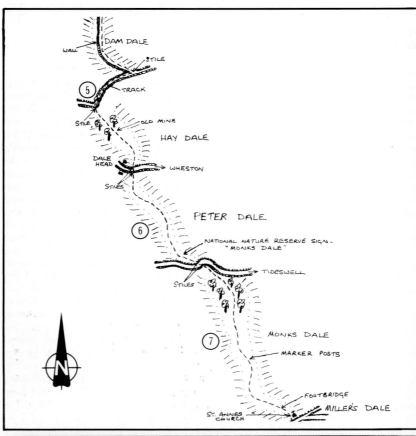

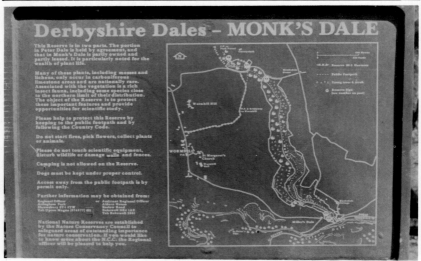

MONK'S DALE NOTICE BOARD

6

Turn left along the A623 road and almost immediately cross the road to the small stile, opposite house No. 21 — Kirkland Cottage. The path is defined and the stiles are all maintained as you cross the fields. Once over the brow of the hill you can see Dam Dale Farm ahead. Keep to the left of it via the stiles, thus gaining the path through Dam Dale, with the stone wall on your immediate right. A little over half a mile through the shallow dale you reach a stile and track. Here turn right and walk along this to the next stile on your left and the path through Hay Dale. First you walk through trees, past a lead mine on your left, before more open country. Ascend the stile and cross the minor road to Wheston; ascend the stile and begin walking down Peter Dale. This dale is impressive, with limestone buttresses on either side and a distinct track to follow. In time the dale becomes much wider before entering a small gorge with a National Nature Reserve sign — Monks Dale. Continue ahead to the Tideswell road, two stiles and a further National Nature Reserve sign. You are now in Monks Dale. The path is rocky and muddy through the trees for the first ten minutes, then you begin ascending up the lefthand side of the dale following marker posts. You keep your high level path as you contour round the dale above the river. Descend to the river and footbridge. Bear left up the right of the dale on a track. At the top descend the walled tarmaced path to reach the road at Miller's Dale beside St. Anne's Church.

MONK'S DALE

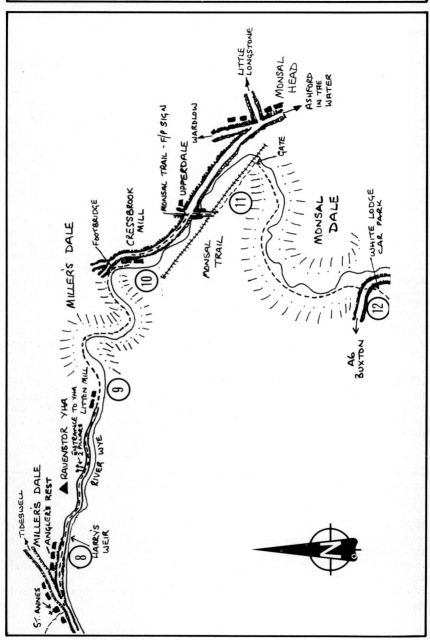

MILLER'S DALE TO MONYASH — 7 MILES

WALKING INSTRUCTIONS

Take the Litton Mill signposted road on your right, passing the Angler's Rest Inn on your left. You keep on this single lane road beside the River Wye for the next mile. En route you pass Harry's Weir on your right, the huge limestone buttress of Raven's Tor on your left and the entrance driveway to Ravenstor YHA also on your left. Enter the works of Litton Mill, now on a concessionary path to Cressbrook Mill via Water Cum Jolly. Beyond the mill buildings you keep the River Wye on your right as you follow a wide track through the trees and past many limestone buttresses. Cross a footbridge and follow the track round to your left through Cressbrook Mill. At the road turn right towards Monsal Head; a footpath sign — Monsal Trail — also indicates that you can get onto the trail at Upperdale, half a mile ahead. Keep on the road until you reach Upperdale Farm and turn right, as footpath signposted, and cross the River Wye and follow the road under the bridge of Monsal Trail. On the other side turn left onto the Trail, which you now follow for a short distance to the start of the famous Monsal Viaduct. Here you turn right off the Trail and descend into Monsal Dale. Bear right and follow the wide path through the dale with the River Wye on your left. For the next three quarters of a mile you keep to this path, passing a weir on your left, through open dale and woodland. After half a mile cross a small stream by a stile and ascend to the A6 road.

RAVENS TOR — One of the highest limestone buttresses in Derbyshire. Much of the 200 foot high face is overhanging, and several hard rock climbs wind their way upwards.

LITTON MILL — Cotton Mill built by Ellis Needham in 1782. He was a ruthless man and employed many pauper apprentices. They were ill-treated and many died; in fact, so numerous were they that the burials had to be split between Tideswell and Taddington. Some of the old gears can be seen on the left as you enter the factory.

CRESSBROOK MILL — Former cotton-spinning mill built by Sir Richard Arkwright in 1783. The present magnificent Georgian front was built in 1815.

MONSAL TRAIL — Former railway line between Matlock and Buxton. Trains ceased operating and it opened in 1982 as a pedestrian way for eight miles between Bakewell and Chee Dale. There are several long tunnels; these have been closed, and link paths take you round these back onto the Trail. The Trail passes through Chee Dale with the highest limestone buttress in Derbyshire — 270 feet high. The Monsal Viaduct gives even greater appreciation of Monsal Dale.

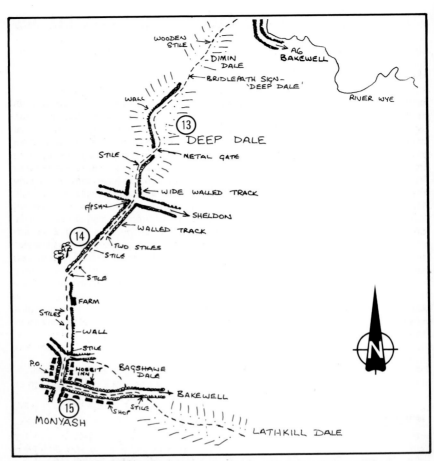

RAVEN'S TOR

10

Cross the road and enter White Lodge car park. Cross the park to the stile on the top lefthand side. Follow the path beyond as it curves around the valley side to the entrance of Deep Dale. Ascend the stile and continue straight ahead up the shallow dale — Dimmin Dale. Just beyond the limestone buttresses you reach a bridlepath sign; turn right following 'Bridlepath to Deepdale'. Once in the dale shortly afterwards turn left and ascend the dale with the wall on your righthand side. After half a mile cross to the other side of the wall via a metal gate close to a bridlepath sign. Continue ahead through a stile to the walled track. Turn left and ascend this to the minor road to Sheldon. Cross the road and as footpath-signposted walk along a walled track. After a quarter of a mile ascend two stiles and keep the stone wall on your right crossing several stiles. Pass a small plantation on your right before bearing left via the stiles to pass on the right of a farm. Keep straight ahead with the wall on your left as you begin descending towards Monyash. The path is defined and well-stiled. Upon reaching the road the footpath sign says — 'Taddington'. Here you have a choice — either continue your dale crossing by crossing the road and following the signposted path to 'Lathkill Dale' or turn right then left immediately and walk along Chapel Street and into central Monyash. At the village green turn left past the Hobbit Inn and shop, and descend the Bakewell road to the entrance of Lathkill Dale and the start of the next stage. If you bypassed the village by walking down Bagshawe Dale you will reach the road at this point.

MONYASH — Once a principal lead mining centre with its own Barmote Court to settle mining disputes. The market cross on the green dates from 1340 when Monyash was given the right to have a market. An annual market is still held here in August. The church dates from the 12th Century and the clock was made by John Whitehurst of Derby in 1805.

LITTON MILL

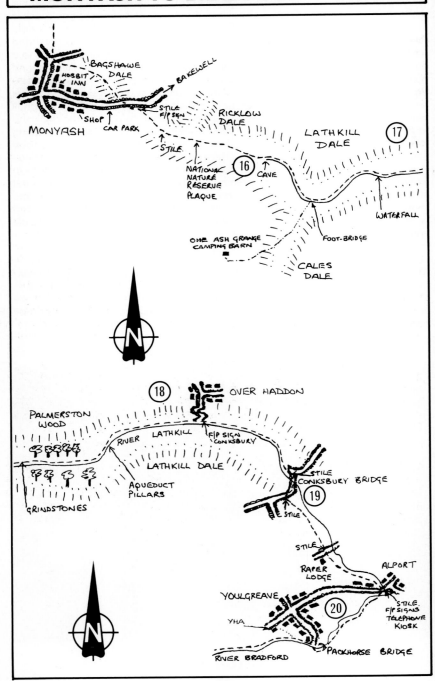

BAGSHAWE DALE

BAKEWELL

HOBBIT INN

BAGSHAWE DALE

STILE F/P SIGN

RICKLOW DALE

LATHKILL DALE

(17)

MONYASH

SHOP

CAR PARK

STILE

NATIONAL NATURE RESERVE PLAQUE

(16)

CAVE

WATERFALL

ONE ASH GRANGE CAMPING BARN

FOOT-BRIDGE

CALES DALE

N

OVER HADDON

(18)

PALMERSTON WOOD

RIVER LATHKILL

F/P SIGN CONKSBURY

LATHKILL DALE

STILE CONKSBURY BRIDGE

GRINDSTONES

AQUEDUCT PILLARS

(19)

STILE

STILE

RAPER LODGE

ALPORT

YOULGREAVE

(20)

STILE. F/P SIGNS TELEPHONE KIOSK

YHA

RIVER BRADFORD

PACKHORSE BRIDGE

N

MONYASH TO BRADFORD — 5 MILES

WALKING INSTRUCTIONS -

From the road half a mile east of Monyash and where the path down Bagshawe Dale gains the road, turn right through the stile and follow the signposted path down into Lathkill Dale. Keep to the dale floor, crossing two stiles before reaching a small gorge and the rubble slope from Ricklow Dale on your left. Just beyond, the dale opens out spectacularly and you reach a National Nature Reserve sign and plaque detailing history notes on the area. Continue ahead down the dale on the distinct path passing the cave on your right where the River Lathkill gushes out. You now walk on the lefthand side of the dale with the river on your right. Continue down the dale over the stiles, passing a small waterfall on your right. Beyond this point the river is quite wide before reaching Palmerston Wood and the remains of a corn mill; the two grindstones can be seen. Enter the wood via the stile close to the National Nature Reserve sign. You now have a wide track to follow, still keeping the river on your right. You keep on this track for the next mile, passing the remains of a lead mine and aqueduct pillars on your left. At the end of the track you reach the narrow road from Over Haddon. Continue ahead past Lathkill Lodge and follow the signposted path — 'Conksbury'. The path hugs the lefthand side of the river; sometimes beside it, sometimes above it and its many weirs. A little over half a mile you reach the road; turn right and cross Conksbury Bridge and its delightful view back to Over Haddon. Follow the road for 250 yards to the next stile on your left. Leave the road here and continue descending across the fields down the rest of Lathkill Dale. The path is well-stiled, and after a quarter of a mile you cross the track close to Raper Lodge. A further quarter of a mile brings you to the road at Alport, opposite a telephone kiosk. Cross the road and descend the track following the path signposted — 'Middleton by Youl-greave' 2 miles. After crossing the River Bradford you walk along a track which is tarmaced further along. All the time the river is on your right. Stiles guide you, and as you near Bradford beneath Youlgreave you pass a small packhorse bridge on your right. Cross the river and turn left and now walk on the right of the river up Bradford Dale.

LATHKILL DALE — The finest dale in the Peak, with steep sides, limestone buttresses, a cave, and the purest water in Britain. The area around Cales Dale is now a National Nature Reserve and was the first in the Peak District, designated in 1972. The Reserve is rich in flowers, with more than 100 species. Remains of lead mining can be seen beneath Over Haddon, especially aqueduct pillars and some buildings of Mandale Mine.

MONSAL DALE WEIR

THE GREEN, MONYASH

LATHKILL DALE BELOW OVER HADDON

BRADFORD TO BIGGIN — 10 MILES

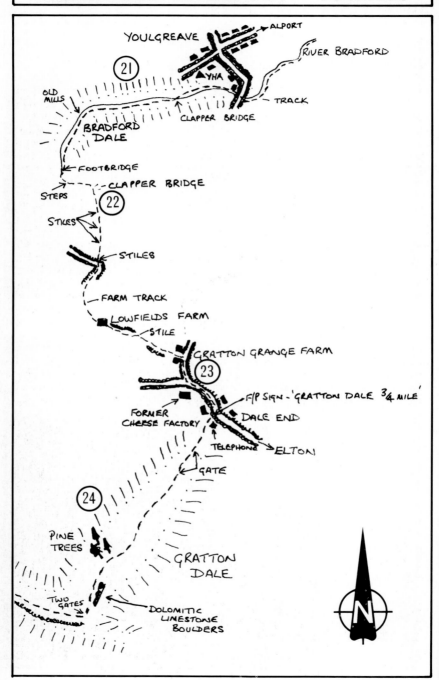

RIVER BRADFORD TO BIGGIN — 10 MILES

WALKING INSTRUCTIONS -

Keep to the righthand side of the river to a clapper bridge and narrow lane from Youlgreave. Part way along this path the ascending tarmaced path on your right into Youlgreave will bring you to the Youth Hostel where a Limey Way register is kept. Cross the clapper bridge and follow the path on the left of the river and past several large fish-ponds. In time the path becomes a track through the woodland. Half a mile from the clapper bridge you reach the remains of a water mill and the track to Middleton. Here you cross the river and turn left, keeping the now infant river on your left. The path is well defined, and you soon cross a small footbridge before ascending steps to some pine trees. Here turn right on the path and descend to the river and cross it via a clapper bridge. Just over the brow of the field you can see the next stile, and the faint path leads you to it and on to the subsequent stiles. Upon reaching the farm track to Lowfields Farm, turn left and follow the track to the farm. Walk through the farmyard to the metal gate. Go through this and keep straight ahead across the field with the wall on your left. Pass through a stile on your left, and now keep the wall on your right as you head for Gratton Grange Farm. As you near the farm buildings you pass through two gates. Walk through the farmyard to the road, passing a barn on your right built in 1853. At the road turn right, and at the road junction in front of a large building — a former cheese factory — turn left for the hamlet of Dale End. 300 yards later, at Dale End Farm, turn right beside the telephone kiosk and follow the signposted footpath — Gratton Dale 3/4 mile. Pass through two gates and keep straight ahead for the one and a half miles through Gratton Dale. After a mile you walk beneath a small pine plantation and weave your way along the dale floor through the dolomitic limestone boulders. At the end of the dale go through a gate and through another immediately on your right and into Long Dale.

FORMER CHEESE FACTORY, DALE END

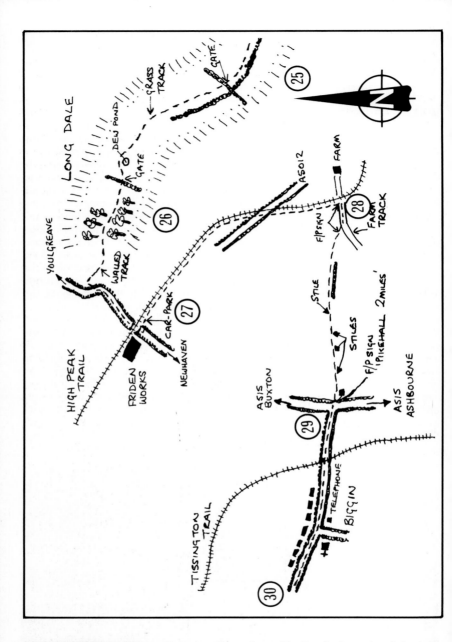

HIGH PEAK TRAIL — Former railway line with nine inclines that linked the Cromford Canal at Cromford Wharf with the Peak Forest Canal at Whaley Bridge 33 miles away. The line was constructed in 1830 at a cost of £180,000. Trains ceased operating in 1967, and in 1972 17 miles of the line was opened as a pedestrian way. The Trail includes the impressive Minninglow embankment and the Gotham curve which has a radius of only 55 yards.

Keep the wall on your left as you walk along a grass track in the shallow long dale. After half a mile go through a gate on your left, still keeping the wall on your left. Walk round the righthand side of a dew pond to reach a gate in the stone wall. Continue ahead along the dale floor with walled woodland on either side of you. At the end of the woodland on your left, leave the dale floor and walk along a walled track on your left to the head of the dale and the road from Friden. The path turns sharp left at the road. Turn left and walk up the road to Friden Works and the High Peak Trail. Pass under the railway bridge before turning left into Friden car park. Once on the trail turn right and follow the trail for the next one and a quarter miles, en route crossing the A5012 road. A quarter of a mile from this road leave the trail at the Concessionary Footpath sign and walk up the farm track to your right. As you reach the first stone wall on your right, leave the track as signposted and follow the path on the righthand side of the wall. Ascend the field beyond the end of the wall to the stile. From here the pathline is faint as you cross the fields using several stiles. After three more stiles you walk through a field gate beside a dew pond before reaching a stile in the corner of the field. Here you descend to the righthand side of a solitary house. The footpath sign says — 'Pikehall 2 miles' — and the stiles take you down the driveway to the A515 road. Cross the road and follow the minor road to Parwich, en route walking underneath the railway bridge of the Tissington Trail. Walk into central Biggin past the telephone kiosk on your left and the Waterloo Inn on your right.

WATERLOO INN, BIGGIN

19

BIGGIN TO THORPE — 8 MILES

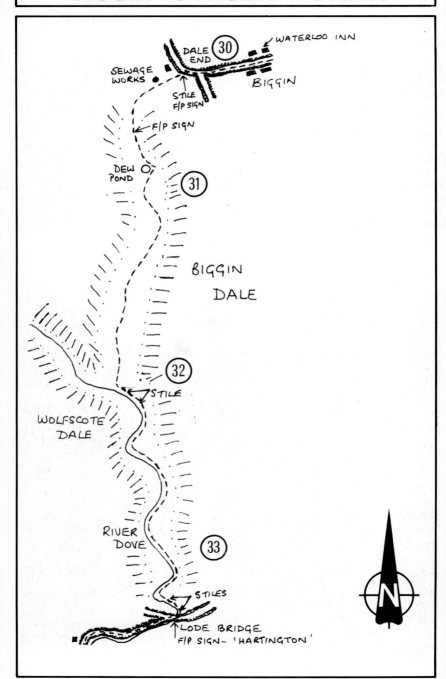

WATERLOO INN

DALE END (30)

BIGGIN

SEWAGE WORKS

STILE F/P SIGN

F/P SIGN

DEW POND (31)

BIGGIN DALE

(32) STILE

WOLFSCOTE DALE

RIVER DOVE (33)

STILES

LODE BRIDGE
F/P SIGN— 'HARTINGTON'

N

BIGGIN TO THORPE — 8 MILES

WALKING INSTRUCTIONS -

Continue along the road through Biggin past the Waterloo Inn and Biggin Hall Farm to Dale End. Here, as footpath-signposted, turn left through the stile and begin the descent into Biggin Dale and the final dale system. First you pass a small sewerage works on your right before reaching a stile and footpath sign. Continue down the dale floor, walking round the lefthand side of a dew pond to a bridlepath sign and National Nature Reserve sign — 'Biggin Dale'. Turn right and descend the dale, and a little over a mile later you reach the River Dove and Wolfscote Dale. Here turn left on the well-used path with the River Dove on your right. For the next one and a half miles you keep beside the river to the road, bridge and house at Lode Bridge. Turn right over the bridge and left immediately down the road to Milldale village and the River Dove on your left. The village is the last one before Thorpe, and has toilets, shop, teas and telephone. Here you can fortify yourself for the final miles.

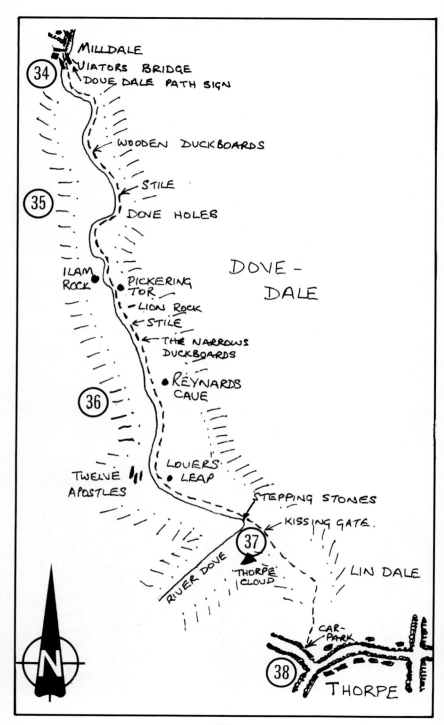

MILLDALE
VIATORS BRIDGE
DOVE DALE PATH SIGN

34

WOODEN DUCKBOARDS

STILE

DOVE HOLES

35

DOVE-DALE

ILAM ROCK

PICKERING TOR
LION ROCK
STILE
THE NARROWS
DUCKBOARDS

REYNARDS CAVE

36

LOVERS LEAP

TWELVE APOSTLES

STEPPING STONES

KISSING GATE

37

THORPE CLOUD

LIN DALE

RIVER DOVE

CAR-PARK

38

THORPE

N

22

Cross Viators Bridge over the River Dove and follow the signposted path along the lefthand side of the River Dove into Dove Dale. After three quarters of a mile you reach Dove Holes — two large shallow limestone caves on your left. A quarter of a mile later you reach Ilam Rock — a 120 ft. high limestone pinnacle on the right bank of the river. Next you walk beneath a large block high up, known as the Watchtower, and the famous Lion Rock. Beyond you enter the 'Narrows' — a duckboarded path above the River Dove where the dale sides are only separated by the swirling water. Shortly afterwards on your left is the impressive limestone archway and Reynards Cave. Continue on the path which now ascends to the top of Lover's Leap providing views down onto the wooded dale. Descend back to the river and a quarter of a mile later reach the stepping stones. Here you turn left through the stile, then a kissing gate, and start ascending the final dale — Lin Dale. On the right is Thorpe Cloud. Keep the wall on your right as you ascend.

After a quarter of a mile you reach a small disused quarry on your left, at the top of the hill. Turn right along the track to the car park, toilets, Post Office and Thorpe village — journey's end. Hopefully here waiting for you is your support party!

DOVE DALE — Stunning dale with wooded slopes, limestone buttresses and pinnacles, and flowing River Dove. Ilam Rock is 120 ft. high, and opposite is Pickering Tor. Approaching the 'Narrows', the rock face is the silhouette of a lion, while above is a large block known as the Watch Tower. Reynard's Cave has a huge natural archway in front of it. The vantage point known as Lover's Leap is where a jilted lover in the mid-18th Century jumped to end everything. Alas, her fall was broken by the bushes, and although scratched she survived happily but singly ever after.

THORPE — The church, dedicated to St. Leonard, dates from Norman times. Inside is a Norman tub font, one of only three in Derbyshire, and a tomb to John Millward who died in 1632 aged 82.

WOLFSCOTE DALE

RAVEN'S TOR

24

OLD COG WHEELS, LITTON MILL

MONK'S DALE

AMENITIES GUIDE

	Village	Campsite	YHA Hostel	B&B	Hotel	Inn	Restaurant	Shop	P.O.
CASTLETON	*	*	*	*	*	*	*	*	*
PEAK FOREST			*		*		*	*	
MILLERS DALE		*	*		*				
MONYASH	*	*	*		*		*	*	
YOUL-GREAVE		*	*		*	*	*	*	*
BIGGIN			*		*		*		
MILLDALE	*		*			*	*		
THORPE	*		*		*				

26

LIST OF INNS

CASTLETON — CASTLE HOTEL
GEORGE HOTEL
OLD CHESHIRE CHEESE HOTEL
THE PEAK HOTEL
YE OLD NAGS HEAD HOTEL

PEAK FOREST — DEVONSHIRE ARMS

MILLER'S DALE — ANGLER'S REST

MONYASH — HOBBIT INN

BIGGIN — WATERLOO INN

THORPE — PEVERIL OF THE PEAK HOTEL
DOG AND PARTRIDGE HOTEL

BED AND BREAKFAST

ASHBOURNE — The Clifton Hotel, Station Road, Ashbourne, DE6 1AA. Tel. 3330.

ASHFORD-IN-THE-WATER — (Bakewell) — Mrs. A. Rowland, Chy-an-Dour, Hillcross, Ashford-in-the-Water, Bakewell, DE4 1QL.
Tel. Bakewell 3162.

BAKEWELL — Mrs C.A. Wilson, Riversdene, Granby Croft, Bakewell. DE4 1ET.

HARTINGTON — Mrs. B. Blackburn, Bank House, Market Place, Hartington, SK17 OAL.
Tel. Hartington 465.

- Mrs. M. Wain, Knowle Cottage, Market Place, Hartington. Tel. Hartington 435

LITTON — Mr. & Mrs. Radford, Hall Farm House, Litton, SK17 8QP. Tel. Tideswell 871124

MONSAL HEAD — Mrs. J. Pennington, Cliffe House Private Hotel, Monsal Head, Derbyshire.
Tel. Great Longstone 376.

- Castle Cliffe Private Hotel, Monsal Head, Derbyshire. Tel. Great Longstone 258.
- Monsal Head Hotel. Tel. Gt. Longstone 250.

MONYASH — Lea Hurst, Monyash, Derbyshire. Tel. Bakewell 2575.
- The Hobbit Inn, Monyash, Bakewell, Tel. Bakewell 2372

THORPE — Mrs. B. Challinor, The Old Orchard, Stoney Lane, Thorpe.
Tel. Thorpe Cloud 410.

- Mr. & Mrs. Everitt, Hillcrest House, Dovedale, Thorpe.
Tel. Thorpe Cloud 436/370.

YOULGREAVE — M. Shinwell, Church Farm, Youlgreave. Tel. Youlgreave 305.

YOUTH HOSTELS — on or close to route.

CASTLETON — Castleton Hall, Market Place, Castleton, Sheffield, S30 2WG. Tel. Hope Valley 20235.

RAVENSTOR — (3/4 mile from route) — **Ravenstor, Millers Dale,** Buxton, Derbyshire, SK17 8SS.
Tel. Tideswell (0298) 871826.

BAKEWELL — (4 miles off route) — **Fly Hill, Bakewell,** Derbyshire, DE4 1DN. Tel. Bakewell 2313.

YOULGREAVE — Fountain Square, Youlgreave, Bakewell, Derbys.
DE4 1UR. Tel. Youlgreave (0629 86) 518.

ELTON — (3/4 mile off route) — **Elton Old Hall, Main St.,** Elton, Matlock, Derbyshire, DE4 2BW.
Tel. Winster (0629-88) 394.

HARTINGTON — (1¼ miles off route) — **Hartington Hall,** Hartington, Buxton, Derbyshire, SK17 0AT.
Tel. Hartington (0298 84) 223.

ILAM — (1½ miles off route) — **Ilam Hall, Ashbourne,** Derbyshire, DE4 2AZ.
Tel. Thorpe Cloud (0335 29) 212.

CAMPING BARN — (1 mile off route) — A converted barn to hut type accomodation, with bed space and cooking facilities at One Ash Grange, above Cales Dale -
close to Lathkill Dale and Monyash. Details and bookings to — Peak National Park Study Centre, Losehill Hall, Castleton, Derbyshire. S30 2WB.

CAMPING SITES — within 2 miles of the route.

CASTLETON — Losehill Caravan Club Site
G.R. SK154834
Tel. Hope Valley 30516

- Rowter Farm on Old Moor.
G.R. SK132822

MONYASH — Haddon Grove Camping Site,
Monyash Road (B5055)
G.R. SK176661
Tel. Bakewell 2343

ALPORT — Greenfields Farm
G.R. SK223636
Tel. Youlgreave 729

NEWHAVEN — Caravan and Camping Park
G.R. SK170602
Tel. Hartington 300

ASHBOURNE — Sandybrook Hall
G.R. SK182482
Tel. Ashbourne 42679

FULWOOD ROCK, BRADFORD DALE

Random lists of the more common birds and flowers to be seen en route:-

BIRDS

Tree-creeper
Wren
Nuthatch
Blue Tit
Wheatear
Curlew
Blackbird
Mallard
Tufted Duck
Little Owl
Robin
Redstart
Sedge Warbler
Redpoll
Swallow
Pied Wagtail

Great Tit
Moorhen
Kingfisher
Coot
Dipper
Grey Wagtail
Raven
Lapwing
Fieldfare
Lesser Black Backed Gull
Marsh Tits
Bullfinch
Hawfinch
Wood Pigeon
Whitethroat
Yellowhammer

DEEP DALE

FLOWERS

Meadow Cranesbill
Kidney Vetch
Ragged Robin
Ramsons
Eyebright
Knapweek
Gorse
Oxtongue
Blackthorn
Wood Sorrel
Birdsfoot Trefoil
Ox-Eye Daisy
Ground Ivy
Monkey Flower
Goatsbeard
Crosswort
Twayblade
Limestone Fern
Bloody Cranesbill
Yellow Archangel
Primrose
Sheep's Fescue
Great Hairy Willow-herb
Mountain Melick
Devil's Bit Scabious
Red Campion
Greater Burnet
Carline Thistle
Foxglove
Cowslip
Bell Flower
Musk Thistle
Jacob's Ladder
Bugle
Thyme
Scurvygrass
Tufted Vetch
Rough Hawkbit
Small Scabious

Rosebay Willow-herb
Dog's Mercury
Rock Rose
Lady's Smock
Wood Anemone
Clustered Bell Flower
Hawkweek
Butterbur
Grass of Parnassus
Marsh Marigold
Herb Robert
Germander Speedwell
Yellow Stonecrop
Wood Forget-Me-Not
Hart's Tongue Fern
Rattle
Lesser Meadow Rue
White Dead Nettle
Bluebell
Mossy Saxifrage
Meadow Buttercup
Lily of the Valley
Slender Bedstraw
Watercress
Wood Sage
Milkwort
Lesser Celandine
Globe Flower
Saxifrage
Nettle-leaved Clover
Early Purple Orchid
Stitchwort
Marjoram
Mountain Pansies
Dog Rose
Harebell
Male Fern
Coltsfoot

LOG

Date ....

TIME STARTED........................... **TIME COMPLETED** ....

Route Point	Mile No.	Arr.	Dep.	Comments/Weather
Castleton	0			
Cave Dale	1/2			
Old Moor	1½			
Old Dam	3			
Peak Forest	3½			
Dam Dale	4½			
Hay Dale	5			
Peter Dale	6			
Monk's Dale	7			
Miller's Dale	8			
Litton Mill	9			
Cressbrook Mill	10			
Monsal Dale	11			
A6	12			
Deep Dale	13			
Monyash	15			
Bagshawe Dale	15			
Lathkill Dale	16			
Alport	20			
Bradford	20½			
Bradford Dale	21			
Lowfield Farm	22½			
Dale End	23½			
Gratton Dale	24			
Long Dale	25			
Friden Station	27			
High Peak Trail	28			
Biggin	29½			
Biggin Dale	31			
Wolfscote Dale	32			
Milldale	34			
Dove Dale	36			
Lin Dale	37			
Thorpe	38			

TRAIL PROFILE

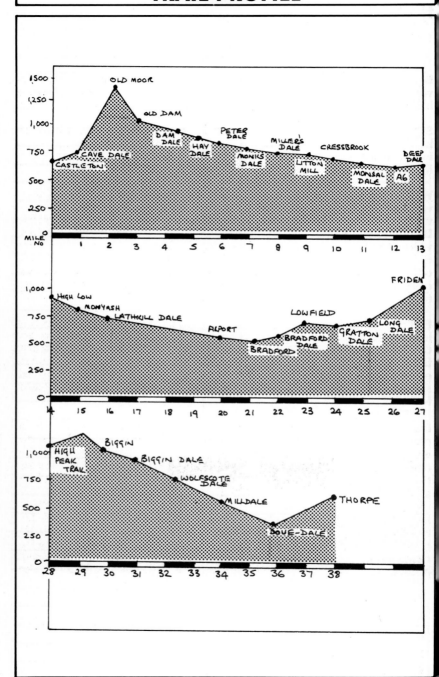

34

EQUIPMENT NOTES — some personal thoughts

BOOTS — preferably with a full leather upper, of medium weight, with a vibram sole. I always add a foam cushioned insole to help cushion the base of my feet.

SOCKS — I generally wear two thick pairs as this helps minimise blisters. The inner pair are of loop stitch variety and approximately 80% wool. The outer are a thick rib pair of approximately 80% wool.

WATERPROOFS — for general walking I wear a T shirt or shirt with a cotton wind jacket on top. You generate heat as you walk and I prefer to layer my clothes to avoid getting too hot. Depending on the season will dictate how many layers you wear. In soft rain I just use my wind jacket for I know it quickly dries out. In heavy downpours I slip on a neoprene lined cagoule, and although hot and clammy it does keep me reasonably dry. Only in extreme conditions will I don overtrousers, much preferring to get wet and feel comfortable.

FOOD — as I walk I carry bars of chocolate, for they provide instant energy and are light to carry. In winter a flask of hot coffee is welcome. I never carry water and find no hardship from not doing so, but this is a personal matter! From experience I find the more I drink the more I want and sweat. You should always carry some extra food such as Kendal mint cake, for emergencies.

RUCKSACKS — for day walking I use a climbing rucksac of about 40 litre capacity and although it leaves excess space it does mean that the sac is well padded, with an internal frame and padded shoulder straps. Inside apart from the basics for the day I carry gloves, balaclava, spare pullover and a pair of socks.

MAP & COMPASS — when I am walking I always have the relevant map — preferably the 1:25,000 scale — open in my hand. This enables me to constantly check that I am walking the right way. In case of bad weather I carry a compass, which once mastered gives you complete confidence in thick cloud or mist.

REMEMBER AND OBSERVE THE COUNTRY CODE

* Enjoy the countryside and respect its life and work.

* Guard against all risk of fire.

* Fasten all gates.

* Keep your dogs under close control.

* Keep to public paths across farmland.

* Use gates and stiles to cross fences, hedges and walls.

* Leave livestock, crops and machinery alone.

* Take your litter home — pack it in, pack it out.

* Help to keep all water clean.

* Protect wildlife, plants and trees.

* Take special care on country roads.

* Make no unnecessary noise.

LATHKILL DALE N.N.R. NOTICE BOARD

THE HIKER'S CODE

* Hike only along marked routes — do not leave the trail.

* Use stiles to climb fences; close gates.

* Camp only in designated campsites.

* Carry a light-weight stove.

* Leave the Trail cleaner than you found it.

* Leave flowers and plants for others to enjoy.

* Keep dogs on a leash.

* Protect and do not disturb wildlife.

* Use the trail at your own risk.

* Leave only your thanks — take nothing but photographs.

LATHKILL DALE CAVE

THE LIMEY WAY

Badges are 3" in diameter with an embroidered walking boot.
If completed within 24hrs a red cloth; 48hrs a green cloth.

BADGE ORDER FORM

Date completed ....

Time ....

NAME ....

ADDRESS ....

....

Price: £2.00 each including postage, VAT and signed completion
certificate.

From: J.N.M. Publications, Winster, Matlock, Derbyshire, DE4
2DQ
Tel: Winster (062988) 454 — (24hrs). FAX: 062988 416

********* You may photocopy this form if needed ********

THE JOHN MERRILL WALK BADGE — walk this route twice or
complete another John Merrill's challenge walk and send details and cheque/PO for £2.00 for a special circular four colour
embroidered walk badge. Price includes postage and VAT.

OTHER CHALLENGE WALKS BY JOHN N. MERRILL -

DAY CHALLENGES -

John Merrill's White Peak Challenge Walk — 25 miles.
Circular walk from Bakewell involving 3,600 feet of ascent.

John Merrill's Dark Peak Challenge Walk — 24 miles.
Circular walk from Hathersage involving 3,300 feet of ascent.

John Merrill's Staffordshire Moorlands Challenge Walk — 26 miles.
Circular walk from Oakamoor involving 2,200 feet of ascent.

John Merrill"s Yorkshire Dales Challenge Walk — 23 miles.
Circular walk from Kettlewell involving 3,600 feet of ascent.

John Merrill's North Yorkshire Moors Challenge Walk — 24 miles.
Circular walk from Goathland — a seaside bash — involving 2,000 feet of ascent.

The Little John Challenge Walk — 28 miles.
Circular walk from Edwinstowe in Sherwood Forest — Robin Hood country.

Peak District End to End Walks.
1. Gritstone Edge Walk — 23 miles down the eastern edge system.
2. Limestone Dale Walk — 24 miles down the limestone dales from Buxton to Ashbourne.

Forthcoming titles —

John Merrill's Snowdonia Challenge Walk.

The Rutland Water Challenge Walk.

John Merrill's Staffordshire Challenge Walk.

MULTIPLE DAY CHALLENGE WALKS -

The Limey Way — 40 miles
Down twenty limestone dales from Castleton to Thorpe in the Peak District.

The Peakland Way — 100 miles.
John Merrill's classic walk around the Peak District.

The River's Way — 43 miles.
Down the five main river systems of the Peak District, from Edale, the end of the Pennine Way, to Ilam.

Peak District High Level Route — 90 miles
Circular walk from Matlock taking in the highest and remotest parts of the Peak District.

COASTAL WALKS —

The Isle of Wight Coast Path — 77 miles.
Complete encirclement of a magnificent island.

Forthcoming books -

The Cleveland Way

The Pembrokeshire Coast Path.

OTHER BOOKS BY JOHN N. MERRILL PUBLISHED BY JNM PUBLICATIONS

DAY WALK GUIDES -

SHORT CIRCULAR WALKS IN THE PEAK DISTRICT
LONG CIRCULAR WALKS IN THE PEAK DISTRICT
CIRCULAR WALKS IN WESTERN PEAKLAND
SHORT CIRCULAR WALKS IN THE STAFFORDSHIRE MOORLANDS
SHORT CIRCULAR WALKS AROUND THE TOWNS AND VILLAGES OF THE PEAK DISTRICT
SHORT CIRCULAR WALKS AROUND MATLOCK
SHORT CIRCULAR WALKS IN THE DUKERIES
SHORT CIRCULAR WALKS IN SOUTH YORKSHIRE
SHORT CIRCULAR WALKS AROUND DERBY
SHORT CIRCULAR WALKS AROUND BAKEWELL
SHORT CIRCULAR WALKS AROUND BUXTON
SHORT CIRCULAR WALKS AROUND NOTTINGHAMSHIRE
SHORT CIRCULAR WALKS ON THE NORTHERN MOORS
40 SHORT CIRCULAR PEAK DISTRICT WALKS
SHORT CIRCULAR WALKS IN THE HOPE VALLEY

INSTRUCTION & RECORD -

HIKE TO BE FIT ....STROLLING WITH JOHN
THE JOHN MERRILL WALK RECORD BOOK

CANAL WALK GUIDES -

VOL ONE — DERBYSHIRE AND NOTTINGHAMSHIRE
VOL TWO — CHESHIRE AND STAFFORDSHIRE
VOL THREE — STAFFORDSHIRE
VOL FOUR — THE CHESHIRE RING
VOL FIVE — LINCOLNSHIRE & NOTTINGHAMSHIRE
VOL SIX — SOUTH YORKSHIRE
VOL SEVEN — THE TRENT & MERSEY CANAL

DAY CHALLENGE WALKS -

JOHN MERRILL'S WHITE PEAK CHALLENGE WALK
JOHN MERRILL'S YORKSHIRE DALES CHALLENGE WALK
JOHN MERRILL'S NORTH YORKSHIRE MOORS CHALLENGE WALK
PEAK DISTRICT END TO END WALKS
THE LITTLE JOHN CHALLENGE WALK
JOHN MERRILL'S LAKELAND CHALLENGE WALK
JOHN MERRILL'S STAFFORDSHIRE MOORLAND CHALLENGE WALK
JOHN MERRILL'S DARK PEAK CHALLENGE WALK

MULTIPLE DAY WALKS -

THE RIVERS' WAY
PEAK DISTRICT HIGH LEVEL ROUTE
PEAK DISTRICT MARATHONS
THE LIMEY WAY
THE PEAKLAND WAY

COAST WALKS -

ISLE OF WIGHT COAST WALK
PEMBROKESHIRE COAST PATH
THE CLEVELAND WAY

HISTORICAL GUIDES -

DERBYSHIRE INNS
HALLS AND CASTLES OF THE PEAK DISTRICT & DERBYSHIRE
TOURING THE PEAK DISTRICT AND DERBYSHIRE BY CAR
DERBYSHIRE FOLKLORE
LOST INDUSTRIES OF DERBYSHIRE
PUNISHMENT IN DERBYSHIRE
CUSTOMS OF THE PEAK DISTRICT AND DERBYSHIRE
WINSTER — A VISITOR'S GUIDE
ARKWRIGHT OF CROMFORD
TALES FROM THE MINES by GEOFFREY CARR
PEAK DISTRICT PLACE NAMES by MARTIN SPRAY

JOHN'S MARATHON WALKS -

TURN RIGHT AT LAND'S END
WITH MUSTARD ON MY BACK
TURN RIGHT AT DEATH VALLEY
EMERALD COAST WALK

COLOUR GUIDES -

THE PEAK DISTRICT .... Something to remember her by.

SKETCH BOOKS — by John Creber

NORTH STAFFORDSHIRE SKETCHBOOK

CALENDARS

1989 JOHN MERRILL PEAK DISTRICT WALK A MONTH CALENDAR

Notes –

44